Border
Vista

# About the Lexi Rudnitsky First Book Prize in Poetry

The Lexi Rudnitsky First Book Prize in Poetry is a collaboration between Persea Books and The Lexi Rudnitsky Poetry Project. It sponsors the annual publication of a collection by a female-identifying poet who has yet to publish a full-length poetry book.

Lexi Rudnitsky (1972–2005) grew up outside of Boston. She studied at Brown University and Columbia University, where she wrote poetry and cultivated a profound relationship with a lineage of women poets that extends from Muriel Rukeyser to Heather McHugh. Her own poems exhibit both a playful love of language and a fierce conscience. Her writing appeared in *The Antioch Review, Columbia: A Journal of Literature and Art, The Nation, The New Yorker, The Paris Review, Pequod*, and *The Western Humanities Review*. In 2004, she won the Milton Kessler Memorial Prize for Poetry from *Harpur Palate*. Lexi died suddenly in 2005, just months after the birth of her first child and the acceptance for publication of her first book of poems, *A Doorless Knocking into Night* (Mid-List Press, 2006). The Lexi Rudnitsky First Book Prize in Poetry was founded to memorialize her and to promote the type of poet and poetry in which she so spiritedly believed.

## Previous winners of the Lexi Rudnitsky First Book Prize in Poetry

Border
Vista
Poems
Anni Liu
刘安妮

A Karen & Michael Braziller Book

PERSEA BOOKS / NEW YORK

Persea Books, Inc.
90 Broad Street
New York, New York 10004

Library of Congress Cataloging-in-Publication Data

Names: Liu, Anni, author.
Title: Border vista : poems / Anni Liu.
Description: New York : Persea Books, [2022] | "A Karen & Michael Braziller Book" | Summary: "In Border Vista, winner of the 2021 Lexi Rudnitsky First Book Prize in Poetry, Anni Liu intimately narrates experiences of being undocumented, or precariously documented, in America, in poems that move between China and the United States"—Provided by publisher.
Identifiers: LCCN 2021062430 (print) | LCCN 2021062431 (ebook) | ISBN 9780892555451 (paperback) | ISBN 9780892555499 (epub)
Subjects: LCGFT: Poetry.
Classification: LCC PS3612.I925 B67 2022  (print) | LCC PS3612.I925 (ebook) | DDC 811/.6—dc23/eng/20220107
LC record available at https://lccn.loc.gov/2021062430
LC ebook record available at https://lccn.loc.gov/2021062431

Book design and composition by Rita Lascaro
Typeset in Apollo
Manufactured in the United States of America. Printed on acid-free paper.

# Contents

一

二

三

# ARS POETICA IN A DREAM LANGUAGE

I dream my mother / unravels / hair out of my mouth

in English / she asks me / to speak Chinese

coils the hair / into a dark gloss / whorled

in her palm / fluency: I can't / unhear my Chinese

memories in English / does that make them / American

memories / the word ravel / means the same thing

as its opposite / to entangle or disentangle / render

incoherent or make plain / & now / in this dream

she leaves me / to muddle her hair / from my mouth

a thin silk / slick with saliva / I render into shapes

that look nothing / like her / once but no longer

ravel meant to waste / spoil / or destroy a thing

as by pulling / a fabric into threads / if we allow

for *obs.* meanings / then let me / also go back

in time / to the original state / examine at length

or in a hurry / because what is obscure / becomes

obsolete / leaving a thin trail of threads / when I

look back / I see the path / hair-dark & raveling

# DEMOLISHED LANDSCAPE WITH OPEN MOUTH

*for a friend, whose name I no longer remember*

when I was a child my family lived
      in a building six stories tall
            and a field of wild grasses grew in front
and in the field was a well with a heavy iron lid
      that one day opened, left agape

so in the field there came to be a mouth
      with a long throat full of rain, the husks
            of crickets and yellow dust, tiny bodies
the rain overpowered and when the wind blew
      the mouth hollowed with sound

in the field you and I played with our fingers
      pointed into guns, our elbows and knees
            patched in the loose camouflage of dirt
we climbed my father's red motorcycle
      ticking as it cooled by the tall grass

here we rushed and tumbled
      straining against the other as if to break
            through to another life
and in the field the mouth opened
      waiting for you to find it

# THE STORY

I was born in Xĭ'ān, a three-thousand-year-old city encircled by walls.

Before I arrived, my mother visited me in dreams: A girl. My father's hair. My mother's mouth.

She waited, devouring shrimp and green apples.

Seven years later, she left.

My father bought a red motorcycle. It gleamed, gold specks in red enamel.

My grandparents moved into the campus apartment where my mother's books were still stacked, and my father stayed on the other side of town.

> Sun fell through knotted curtains. The moon visited us in turn.

In summer, the road out of campus kicked dirt in our faces. Sweat mixed with dirt made a new and tougher skin.

In winter, motorcycle rides with white cotton face masks and stiff wool coats. The air's silt like snow.

I heard her voice on the telephone: "Where do you miss me?" But I could not locate *missing* in my body.

(Why document this, as if forgetting were the worst thing?)

> The ocean came to my city once, city once mine.

City so dry and ill-equipped that any hard rain will make it flood.

It was no ocean. Just the sky.

If your city floods with streets like asphalt river beds, carry your child to piano lesson on your back. Wear shower slippers, the only waterproof shoes you own. Be prepared for nails. A long nail. The arch of the foot.

Another time: me fevered for days, my mother gone,

my father took me to work. He spread couch cushions on the office floor for me to lie on, asked me what I needed.

"Tell me a story," I said.

He never told stories, but that day, he told me this:

It has a happy ending. The bunnies find their way home to their mother.

But her eyes, exhausted of tears, fall to the ground. Trees spring up where they land, trees with eyes in their bark.

My mother never came back. Instead, I went to her, to Ohio and lead skies.

After the story was over—the rabbits sheltered under the eye trees—my father covered me with a thin blanket.

I had fallen asleep.

He could go back to work.

# AFTERSHOCK

When the earthquake shimmers through the city, she is peeling an apple in her husband's sixth-story apartment. The trembling lasts for three seconds. Jarred, she nicks her thumb with the knife. White flesh, red skin—the clarity of injury. The apartment remains unchanged around her: light bleaching the blank walls from which nothing fell, cold white tiles glinting under her slippers, and by the door, beside the other lumped shoes, her black leather pumps. In the kitchen, she rinses her hands. The cut is small yet deep. Blood muddies the sink. From the window she can see the street beyond the gate, and there, her husband, bringing their daughter home from piano lesson like any other Saturday. Biting into the apple, she tastes her own blood.

# MEMORY IN A FOREIGN LANGUAGE

weekday afternoons I walk from school to the English
       class in the foreign       language university

           the air is the color of amber       or it is only
this way in memory       which has stained it
       like a film       remastered

       here I learn a language       is the way someone you love
looks when speaking it       and English is my mother

moving her face in ways she does not at home
long pursed O's       wide smile       that's almost a grimace

the lesson underway:       *sounds with the letter L*
       I mimic the sounds       my voice swallowed     by the class

I stretch       my mouth and feel the shape of what
       I don't yet understand       chanting     *lack*

       *luck*   *lock*     *lack*   *luck*
                   *lock*     and what happens next

I don't remember yet

# BĚIJĪNG AQUARIUM

At the entrance, the one-note blue of an oceanic
mural, landlocked in gray cement blocks. I hover
by the door, wanting and not wanting
to go in. This double-edged feeling is new,
pleasures having been purely pleasurable
just days before: assorted dinosaur erasers,
a neon plastic pellet gun, sharing a coke
with my dad at the park, and the last bite
of every red bean bun Yéye brought home.
But here, in Běijīng, with my other grandparents,
I am suddenly shy, and guilty in my shyness.
For the camera I fake smile after smile. I miss
Năinai and Yéye and my bed's white lace comforter
under which Black Dog would have to sleep
without me. Inside the eerily empty aquarium,
I begin to notice a gray glint sinking, a plumb line
dowsing my body. I look through the thick-walled tanks
at fish slinking through the water, skirting
the white eyes of the spotlights, and feel
my personality clamp around me like a hand.
At the end of the tour, the dolphin room
is closed, the late show long over, and this last
disappointment is almost too much to bear.
I press my nose against the glass to hide my face
and from the cloudy depth a blue curve emerges
and approaches the glass in all her blue
length and looks me in the eyes, her mouth open
as if in greeting, before diving back, corkscrewing
the water as she vocalizes something I recognize
as joy. She comes three times to where I stand,
her dips and loops in the tank more energetic
each time she returns and I stand riveted
until my grandparents lead me away, worried

I'd disturb the dolphins' rest. She's a performer,
Wàigōng tells me. All day she heaves her great weight
from the blue-dyed tank and into the air
of a thousand human beings cheering. We tell
ourselves when she opens her mouth, she is laughing,
and when she cries out, she is laughing.
Hours later, at the airport, I am led away from
my grandparents and through the gate to fly
to a place called Detroit. There, my mother waits,
deep in the terminal's gray-blue interior.
None of us know that once you pass through the gate
there is no coming back to the entrance, no other chance
to say goodbye. Wàigōng and Wàipó wait for two hours
for me to return before they realize I am already in the air.
As the airport and then the city falls away, I put my face
to the window. For the first time, I see the Great Wall
along the spine of mountain, cutting across the landscape.
The American attendants stroll down the aisle
to greet me. Within my silence, I smile and smile.

# DEPARTURE SEQUENCE

From the belly of the plane, led by a stranger,
I was the last one to descend.

Everything happened at a distance
I could see but do not feel.

I had not been aware
of suffering. All I had
done was sit.

So much of life
just happens.

Before I leave, Lǎolao lacquers my nails
with polish that catches
and holds the light.

After months of living under the cloudless American sky,
the clear polish yellows like the pages of a book
left open, exposed.

My foreignness, a name
that others used
to know me by.

But all of you were indistinguishable, too,
by which I mean and do not mean
to compare you to burning.

In the Hunan Buffet, a digital expanse of water
falls shimmering through the TV screen.

With her cup of free tea, my mother rinses away
the meat's pungent sauce. This, the only restaurant
where she will pay to eat.

This is our life now. I stop speaking to her
in Chinese, and no one calls from home.

# WHAT NO ONE TOLD YOU

You will want to go back. Not
right away, perhaps, not as you run
towards the train's open doors

and not during the nightmiles
in which the distance collapses under
the wheels into ordinary darkness,

and maybe not while laid across
the row of empty airplane seats,
the young Chinese couple helping you

order food the first to witness
your foreignness and feel—what?
Pity for what they themselves have been?

Years, maybe, before this urge
to return can be admitted any place
other than your bed, when sleep runs

from you and thoughts of home,
safe in the darkness, return
as you will long to, knowing

and not knowing just how long
the distance stretches while you learn
to live another life with a scavenged

repertoire of days and songs,
the unknowable night ferrying you
farther away all the while.

# AUBADE, UNTROUBLED

I wake up in the AC and eat
what I want: toast, tea, and eggs
sunny-side up. I have my pick
of places to sit and write, shelves
full of books, dusty with want
of touch. On the porch, I water
the mint, basil, and jade—I bend
to greet their dirt. How good
they smell, their crinkled leaves
furry and veined, papery and palmate,
how generous they are to feed me
and house the spiders and mites
teeming their stems, how martian
the efflorescences emerging
between their silent green tongues.
Across the lawn, the pool gleams,
flat and still, yet untroubled
by bodies and shrieks in the dense
June heat, by families burnt with neon
floaties circling its blue eye of relief.
These are the good days.
How much do I need to forget
to keep this smile on my face?

## ADDITIONALLY, WHAT FREEDOMS HAVE
## I BEEN TRAINED TO DENY MYSELF?

Today, there is need for accumulation. For measurement and completion—for reaching.

Today, an inflamed bubble on the tonguetip that I rub against an incisor's edge.

Humble may be your way, but not one will know it.

Slink, if you wish, clinking your scales like tiles in a quake.

After years of studying life forms in the academy, she finally gave up naturalism and allowed the muscles of her arms, back, and legs to make the marks.

What permanence there may have been, elided.

How does it feel, in Indiana?

Simple arithmetic, but conjured at all times like a language.

I don't know if I can tell you anything else about my life.

# BORDER VISTA

*n.: a 10-foot boundary clear-cut into*
*forest for ease of surveillance*

for two years I live within
    a mile of the US/

    Canada border

from the tiny apartment
    I share with D
    and his son R

       we often walk
       down the hill and
       behind the gravel lot

where totaled cars appear
       windowless
       headlights crazed
       from impact
then disappear

       once he and his
bright towheaded
       boy like a blond alarm

cross it without
            thinking

       (and is this the part
       of the story I find
       most unbelievable)

when they turn back
toward home      two barrel-

chested officers wait
on the track

after a few minutes'
questioning being
white Americans
they are free to go

D never mentions it again
but for weeks

washing dishes
vacuuming threadbare carpet
I find myself
in that tunnel
through the woods

and an urge comes
to run
into its leafless
domain and cross over

knowing I would not
be able to come back
if I did

but dying      to be somewhere
else

# NORTHEAST KINGDOM

Summer makes haloes of our faces,
light-chapped as we bathe near the sharp-

lipped rocks, icing our beers in snowmelt.
If we stay, we could make a life for ourselves

in this place named for its dead
ends, its trailers and trucks left gutted

and raw on their sides, half-buried by years
of tall grass. On the farm, a single crimson tree.

The sheep graze, milk-eyed and solemn
as children. We keep our books closed,

not marking time except by the bloom
of mold on the thistle-wrapped cheese

ripening in the cellar's vinegared dark.
At the end of an unmarked trail, you'll find

a lake called Shadow where I swam naked
for the first time, shoulders cloaked in pondweed

and stars. A mile from the border, among the grey-
eyed juncos and cattle, no one knows my name.

# NIGHT SWIM AT SHADOW LAKE

I can barely swim but I don't tell them that.
At the beach, the guys joke about leeches
longer than my hand. They strip

and hoot with pleasure as they leap off
the slick rock. I keep my underwear on,
feel my way in, the rocks first becoming dirt,

then a soft sucking silt. Without my glasses,
the lake surface gleams, oiled with stars.
Someone told me once to imagine the water

holding me up to the air, buoyant,
but all I do is sink. The lake's long fingers
plug my ears, grip me like a hand closing.

Panicked, I plash back to the shallow muck
and wait. In the car back to the farm,
I sit with towel stuffed between my legs.

No one tells any jokes. In the tensed
silence, I realize they'd meant for me
to take off all my clothes. I roll down

my window, let in the night and its shrill
insect trills, its sharp slaps of wind. My entire life,
I have been afraid of the wrong things.

# DOCUMENT: EIGHT MONTHS BEFORE EXPIRATION

To the Kingdom, as to this country, I came with my one bag.

The light along the mountains, our two outlines in the grass.

Is this what is meant by *tragedy*? That you could not do otherwise, despite the knowing.

And so, I stayed.

Scoured thrift shops for clothes my size. Bought my first pieces of furniture, paid too much.

All winter we ate only what the corner store stocked, what our own two hands could gather.

Such pleasure, to learn how much I could do without.

# SIX YEARS OLD, MY CLASSMATES AND I

believe we invented this game of jumping
        from great heights, of punishing our bodies
for their softness. As if, by sustaining enough pain,
        we could be tumbled tough and world-proofed
against hurt. I am young enough to still believe
        that old saying about eating bitterness.

But there is one girl who refuses to play.
        Standing on the edge of the cement stage,
she wears a dress the color of whitefish
        open on a butcher board. The skin on
her face seems brand new, never ruined
        by sun, by exertion, by the gritty yellow dirt.

She would have to learn how to fall.
        The crowd of our classmates gathers beneath us.
Their hard little faces like mine, smeared with snot
        and dirt, our red scarves a knot at our throats.
My hands find her shoulders, pillowy and warm—
        all it takes is one quick shove:

she is free of the stage and sailing,
        pale arms akimbo, soft whimper
of surprise, to land face first against the ground.
        When the teacher reaches her,
asking *who did this to you*, her voice is choked
        full of blood and no one dares say

that it is my name she repeats like a drowned song,
        but I know: it was me, it was me, it was me.

# AFTER SCHOOL

*for R*

You want to be a hunter.
When your dad says *no*

*guns*, you turn to hooks and lines.
Camouflage binoculars hang

heavy from your neck, a compass
swings from your belt loop,

and you never take off
the thick paracord cuffed

to your wrist. In your kit,
florid lures tangle in the neon

line. You want to be like all
the other boys. You amass

a dazzling array of knives.

# AND I LOOKED AWAY

I saw you aim for the squirrel with your slingshot. I saw you shatter a water glass with a yoyo's metallic spin. I saw you sink your treble hook into the bathroom rug. I saw you melt her name into the snow with your fist, saw you in the deserted school parking lot without your coat. I saw you make ten free throws in a row. I saw you miss the autistic boy's head by an inch. I saw you test the knife against your thumb. I saw you bring a pond turtle home in your bookbag, saw you want to keep it. I saw your eyes water when I bring up your mother in her cell. I saw you lift your baby tooth with the tip of your tongue, flip it like a house to its side. I saw you snag a largemouth bass, saw you struggle to unhook its lip, wince, cut the line.

## ... *LOSS AND GRIEF ARE GENERATED BY JURIDICOPOLITICAL MECHANISMS*...

When she told them *he hurt me*
they put him in a cell and gave him
a criminal history. *We will kick him
out of this country but first, let us take
his money, how much do you want?*
She shook her head.
*My daughter*, she said. *I want my
daughter.* Which of course was what
got them here in the first place.
Only now, the fact of him
in a cell meant she could
ask his parents for anything.
The girl's grandparents stayed up
whispering in the dim yellow glow
as the girl slept and woke, shaken
by dreams of fires and kidnapping,
not knowing the worst of what
would happen was already
unfolding, and like the heroine
in any story, she was afraid
but looking in the wrong direction.
When they send her away, the girl believes
she is going on vacation. For safekeeping,
she leaves her best doll behind.

In the new country, she visits her father
in jail. People she does not know
and never see again take them
to eat American Chinese, drive them
to the airport where he will be deported.
At the curb, they watch other people hug goodbye.

He picks her up as if she is still a baby,
as if they are posed before a vista
of rare beauty, as if she is still his to hold.
She smiles automatically for the shutter.
His hands, which, trembling, remind me
of what he did, actions for which this moment
is punishment, for which the next twenty years
of absence is punishment—years during which
no one asks the mother anymore what it is she
wants. Just like no one asked me.

# SLEEPLESSNESS: A HISTORY

An early memory, recurring. I heard and felt from afar my body wailing and pushing its limbs against each other as if to negate them. I heard my mother calling my name, pleading *What's wrong, what's wrong?*—but I could not say. My wails alien even to myself.

\*

In the boarding school dormitory, I slept with the next day's clothes folded next to my face. Watery light spilled in from the hallway. I kneaded pills from the ochre fibers of the sweater Năinai knit.

Late one night, after the other girls were already asleep, my father appeared in the doorway, whispering my name. He led me to a large banquet room filled with men he knew from work, to a seat at an enormous table of unfamiliar delights: frog legs in clear broth, a boat stacked with technicolor fish, deep-fried crickets, and snails stewed in wine. Between conversation and drinks, he ladled delicacies onto my plate. When he returned me to the dormitory bed, I was already dreaming.

\*

For a year during middle school, my mother and I lived in a one-bedroom apartment. I had a bunk bed in a corner of the room that was kitchen, dining room, and living room. Some nights I'd be jostled out of sleep by the light coming on, or by the toaster's bright *ding*, and, in a blink of wakefulness, see my mother at the table, bent over a small plate of food. Her aloneness so complete I felt ashamed to witness it. When asked, she told me it was hunger. Hunger woke her, as it had always done.

\*

In high school, after my mother left for the night shift, I'd lie in bed with all the lights on, alert to every rustle and creak. I was too old to be scared of the dark, but still I listened. Through the walls, I felt the locust trees grow deeper into the dirt, and learned what the moles taste in the patient porous earth. All night, I'd sleep and wake, sleep and wake— each time thinking that morning had come.

# DITCH

For a creek, I had the drainage ditch
dug behind the row of streets. In it:
Mtn Dew bottles half full of piss, party
balloons, tadpoles and toads, splinters
of fish. Someone claimed they saw
a turtle and I spent a whole week wading
against the current, shins slathered
with leaves, looking, and seeing instead
a snake slip across a rock like rain.
If you walk along the ditch's grassy banks
from here, it will take you back to
Second Street, then Scott Hamilton
(the name a mystery to me for years),
to those first places I called home
in this country. One has a balcony that,
when it was ours, held nothing but air.
The one on Second is street level, shuttered,
but I know what it's like inside:
nubby carpet that sandpapers bare feet,
the walls damp with shower steam
and nothing ever dries, this place where
I first learned to be scared of being alone,
where I buried my first bird. The ditch
will take you all the way back to my old
elementary school, the track (eight loops
of which make one mile), and the rusty
hinges of the swings where, after school,
no one as witness but the crows, my mother
confessed she didn't know how to swing.
So if you saw us there, hurtling through
the late fall day, gripping our chains,
racing each other to the top, you would

never guess it was me who taught her
how to become your own engine of push
and pull, how to give your body to air.

# QÌGŌNG

we enter
as if through a door
       the woods

the red pines
       sway over us
affected by a different air

*let your breath empty*
       *from the diaphragm*
I lean to catch his voice

*through lips lightly parted*
*tongue touching*
       *the roof of the mouth*

and after    *look*
*at my palms*    stippled
pink with blood

he lifts them to my face

# REMAINS

Past boarded houses and old cemetery stones
             blank as teeth,

      the railway bridge takes us
over the river.
    October, and soon
           the snows, the long winter

    we're not sure
        we can endure.

On a rot-dark rail-tie:        a scattering
    of bones.
          One the length of my finger,
thin & faded as a day moon.

    An ivory ring,

      the puzzle sequence of spine—
no skull to give

    the creature a face.

*A squirrel* we think, or maybe
    something larger,
          something that struggled

as the hawk tore its pelt.

      Was it drawn to the tracks
    as we are, magnetized

to its heat?    We bury

the bones in our pockets.

Turning toward home
                    we balance
              on the polished rails
that appear—
         in the distance—to meet.

# FINDING FRUIT

There were fruit trees in Xī'ān,
and there are some there even now,
though it's hard to believe

with the smog and construction
and men motoring along the sidewalks
ripping gold earrings right out

of people's ears. Lining the streets
of the Foreign Language University,
trees bore apricots and walnuts

for everyone to eat. Years later,
I found fruit in the Northeast Kingdom
of Vermont: ambushes of blue,

black, and elderberries that ripened
on the tongue. All fall of that year
I walked the crabapple highways

with a bag, lonely for sweetness.
Against my side, the apples rolled, heavy
as the silvery baoding balls my father spun

on slow, sun-dense mornings,
waiting for me to wake, cradling them
in his palm until the metal was warm as skin.

# ON JAY PEAK ROAD

The unplowed road leading to the open field
        can be known only by the line of trees separating it
        from field, from snow, from snow colored sky.

Deer come at night with their cloven hooves,
        carve paths between stunned milkweed
        and crabapple trees still burdened
with dark-pitted fruit.

Crossing a deer-shaped patch of earth,
        I come back to the edge
of an ancient sadness of being
        just one thing.

In the valley, houses and tin-roofed
        churches carve the land
        with shadow as I wait
along the treeline, needing to know

        how long it will take for them to see me
and be afraid, how soon their ribbed flanks
        will tense with recognition.

        I am in hunting country
and have no wish to untrain them of their fear.
Only that we might meet eyes
        across this ice-locked field

and for a moment be alive
        in the same place.

# PERMIT

I learned to drive
in a blizzard.
I was twenty-two
and could finally
legally work my job
at the China Moon
buffet thirty minutes
away from the 2br
where we lived a mile
from the border.
He was thirty-three
in the passenger's seat
of his $800 Forester
saying almost
nothing as I inched
up the snow-thick
road. Who knows
where the asphalt
ended and the woods
began. The packed snow
beneath the tires made
a noise like pressing
and bending the pages
of a book, the sound
of something crushed
against itself. He was
always teaching me
something. Even after
I got licensed, I never
considered driving away.

# SOLSTICE

Here in the North with him, all days
        are cold ones. For weeks I hibernate,
                retreat to this cool inner trunk like a flute

frozen into snow. In the mornings
        the grass is hard with frost, crystal
                in the gray light. I read the classics

and try not to think of Demeter when my mother calls
        asking what every mother asks—*come home*—
                especially when the man is older, has a son,

keeps her daughter in the woods
        of a faraway place. The flip phone only works
                by the single south-facing window.

The longer we talk, the more words
        obscure the view. I say everything
                except his sudden rage, the spit he aimed

at my face that he *didn't mean, didn't mean.*
        Soon, the winter solstice. The winter solace.
                There is a certain solace to be found. Last night,

five stars in a zagged W—
        Cassiopeia, the queen tied
                to her throne. Who is the monster here?

With his poor eyesight, he could only point
        to Sirius. But I could see it all. The dog,
                the queen, the hunter and his gem-bright sword.

# HYPNOGOGIA

Each morning comes with crows hacking at the house with beak and claw, crow-babes in tow.

Crows & their three-knock-caw, bluebirds in the badminton net, starlings iridescing the grass, & in the eaves of your study window, a colony of cliff swallows mouth mud & straw into nest.

*They want us gone*, I think, shivering under damp quilts, his side of the bed hours-empty.

Crow calls echo in the empty house, follow me into dreams.

Flies find their way in, die trapped against the glass, dry black carcasses husking the sill. When I sweep them up their wings come free of their bodies.

When the baby swallows hatch, every adult swallow in the colony takes turns bringing food up from the field.

I take a cup of coffee up to his office, every step loud as a shot in the hollow parts of the house. The light from the window limns the doorway & when I knock I can hear him sigh.

Can the birds see him through the glass at work, shaping words into plays no one will perform?

It is their home we live in, their nesting box of fiberboard & filmy paint. They surround us when we sleep, when we play catch with his son, surround us when our voices rise, when he pins me to the bed & holds me there as if under water & I see lights behind my eyes.

He takes everything: my story, my bread & my body, my trust in the universe. But what, if anything, does he take that I do not readily give?

Outside, chimney swifts wheel above the fallow field, feet so small they cannot land, whole lives spent frenzying the air.

Through the board-thin walls of the house I hear the hatchling swallows, their hunger for everything the world would give.

# SHAPE NOTE

Bread & Puppet Theater

In the Paper Mache Cathedral, a barn
with a packed dirt floor and walls swarming
with thousands of butcher paper people,
their eyes and mouths painted with a rough
brush, open O's just like our own as we face
each other and sing—our own four walls
of sound. We rend the red dams of our throats:
*Am I born to die? To lay this body down?*

We rehearse *Shatterer-of-Worlds Chapel*
*with Naturalization Services for Applicants*
*Requesting Citizenship in the Shattered World*,
shuffle onto the stage behind papier mache bodies
spined with sticks.
                              Am I an applicant
to the shattered world, or one of its permanent
residents? The puppets contain our silence, list
side to side as they're passed between us.
We sway. We raise our arms. We fall
to the ground. *Am I born to die?*

He is at the center of the stage,
cranking the scrap-wood arm
of the windmachine. I fall
at his feet. Here, the dirt is cool, effluvial.
Am I already underground? I reach out
and hold his ankle, the bone and tension of it
in the limbo of blackout.
*And must my trembling spirit*
*fly into a world unknown?*

Two years from now, to end
another argument, he will wrap his hands
where my shoulders meet my neck
to shove me out of bed—

                              is it there, on the floor
of our rented clapboard house, that I will remember
the piano is a percussion instrument—a levered body
that sings when struck?

I am still enthralled by the music
I cannot master, by the humming
opening the keys make
in which the ear finds yearning,
gloom. All I have to do is move
my hand, and hear how it changes—
sweet now, wistful, almost bearable.

四

# UPON HEARING THE NEWS

You stand in a window in the fifth story of a tall concrete
building. The sun heats your face. Below, students
saunter between classes, and the blue shard of sky
each jay carries does not shatter as they flap from tree
to red-struck tree. Clusters of insect debris in the window's
spider web assume the likeness of dark heads bobbing
down the street. A black car slides across the bottom
of your field of vision as if the field of vision itself is sliding
so you wobble a bit on your legs, tighten your grip
on the marble ledge, body rocking back to the memory
of storing squash in the hay of a barn during another late
summer in another place, when, hearing the pigeon's
wing-clap in the rafters, you had looked up, and vertigo
unscrewed the lid of you.

                                        You did not fall.
You closed your eyes to the twirl of light and teetered
on the brink of something awful, hugging the mottled
kabocha against you like an anchor until it passed:
tiny crystals of calcium carbonate were disturbing the cupula
of the inner ear which fired false signals to the brain,
made you think falling when you lay down to rest, falling
when you craned your neck to take in the shape of some shadow
passing above you in the dustlight of a September afternoon.

# IN HER PLACE

It has been almost twenty years, but when
Wàigōng is diagnosed, my mother decides

to move home. Who to clean her apartment,
who to make the arrangements, but me,

with a suitcase always packed and ready
to be elsewhere? While she's gone,

I sleep in her bed, dreaming her dreams
in the fanned dark. I wear the shape of her

days like a cape. In the after-dinner dim,
I walk her route around the neighborhood,

waving back to a stranger who calls me
by her name. In her apartment

ransacked by grief—thief that it is—
I eat from her stores of wood ear,

mung bean, hard grains stocked
for nameless emergencies. In her place,

I can't help but think she will never return,
that she'll leave me to this country, alone.

But mornings, her face greets me in the mirror.
From my mouth, what else but her voice?

# GOING BACK

When she returns, we mostly sit in separate rooms, faces down
into our screens. I hear her leaving him

messages on WeChat. She won't get out of bed, sleeps with her glasses on.
There is no gentle enough way to wake someone

in this much pain. Each time, she comes to with a start, awfulness
dawning—so I let her sleep.

Without us, the hours shift. I pull cold dishes from the fridge and watch
as the heat makes them weep. She doesn't eat.

Bedside, she hands me her phone: there, in shaky footage, her father
walks in the courtyard, leaning hard

into his cane, city wind flapping his trousers like sails around his legs,
honing the edge of our missing so sharp it sings.

After dinner, we start on the usual walk toward my elementary school
and its park, its bright machinery,

but two blocks out she stops, turns around. *Huí qù ba,* she decides,
and so we do, turn and go back—

to the apartment stacked with boxes, her suitcase gaping.
We both know *here* is not what she meant.

# SIGHTINGS

There is no telling today, no warbler
        to darn the rupture
with bright stitches of flight.

Thinking of him and sharp-shinned
hawks calling back and forth
        across the field—*keer keer keer*—

and I wonder, is it arrival or departure
        they announce?

I find a chunk of coal in the road
        etched with pocks and divots
like a lightless moon, hold it sharp-edged

to my eye, and in the blue-tinge
        of its sheen (dead matter
        long compressed in the earth's

damp heat) I can see geese flying,

their thin tracery hung so high
        it is a seam of smoke—
            an imaginary shoreline.

# MISAPPREHENSION

When, seventeen years later, I return, I discover my father

walks faster than I can keep pace, knowing more than I do

about what time means and what distances we must

cross. Seeing him round the lake's edge, as if alone, without

the anomaly of my presence, I want to ask him: Who

taught you to look at a bird? When did you first recognize me

as your own? The first time I lost him was in the market

when I took the hand of a man who was him

until he looked down with another face. I was afraid then,

too. Now I stop on the path.

All the long minutes of my absence materialize, pulse

with each step he takes toward the rest of the world.

Who is abandoning whom?

Strangers pass around me, they to whom I have no obligation.

Now the man that is him stops, too, and not finding

me, makes his way back through the crowd

toward where I wait. When he sees me,

who will I be?

# XĪ'ĀN NOCTURNE WITH JASMINE AND PEARS

I call my mother to tell her about a rare dream
in the first language:

      the fruit vendor's miniature green pears
      the soft juice I crave

      she pays but gets the wrong change
      & I realize she can't read the words
      on the cardboard sign and doesn't know
      how much she is owed

she reminds me that the word for pear
sounds the same as the word for leave
           梨 (lí) and 离 (lí)
you're telling me I paid too great a price
to leave, she says

inflected differently, 莉 (lì) is jasmine
      my mother's namesake

how do I tell her that a week earlier, leaving
my grandparents' home, an ambush of jasmine
stopped me on the sidewalk—small mouths
muted with grime yet still sweet as a rain-
dipped stone
          I plucked one
tucked its velvet trumpet behind my ear

now half a world away
      my mouth empties:
every word sounds the same

# JIĀNGSŪ, EARLY SUMMER

He takes me, his adult child swaddled in foreignness, to the southern provinces.

Opaque scenes unfold, here among people with whom I once belonged.

We walk streets lined with vendors and dappled plane trees.

Everything I reach for, he buys.

I record each parting hour for a while. Lapse into silence.

He is gentler than I remember. Offering me a bowl of zhōu, his hands stumble.

Father, recite this world to me.

    银行 a bank

    鸭血 duck blood

    胡同 alley

Listening, I wipe our distance clean.

# TRANSUBSTANTIATION SONNETS

Most days you can't see the mountains
surrounding our ancient city,
but in any weather you can hear the hiss
of hot oil and the popped rice vendor's
iron kettle cranked in an eternal circle.
Once when I was four and sick, I spent days
sprawled across the cool bamboo mat
until sleep and wake became variations
of heat and filtered light. Năinai tied
red thread to my limbs as if tethering
a balloon to its weight. When the fever broke,
I sat in Yéye's shoe and ate a crescent
of watermelon, leaving glossy teardrop
seeds to stick to his socks all day.

It has been more than twenty years.
None of this exists anymore.
All my old neighborhoods are now
demolished. Where are the bricks
from the courtyard of my childhood
that I ground into powder with a rock?
Bent for hours over discarded remnants,
I was tireless in my task, riveted by it
until called away, palms powder-
stained and satisfied at seeing one thing
become so thoroughly something else.
I can't see the mountains, but most days,
bent and rapt, I am tethered still—
to this dust, to red threads I tie, retie.

# ENTRIES FROM HOTTEST YEAR ON RECORD

1.
Woke up early to write, killed flies instead.

2.
In the pot, I boil bones with huājiāo and fennel, attempting to reproduce a past taste. The result is a gray diluted broth, ghost enough to conjure.

3.
On Facebook you can tag a picture as "my grandmother."

If you hover your mouse over the blue tag, you can see 5,017 pictures of "my grandmother." None of them mine.

4.
The slap of plastic slippers against cement—
how long have I imagined you in your absence?

5.
I remember it will rain today, then look up to see it is already raining.

6.
The season slides to a close.
A woman kneels over a tub of water.
In it, a dark muscle circling.

7.
The question of the relationship between suffering, sorrow, and sorriness—what equation could be formed, if any?

8.
Microsoft wants to correct my uncertainties. When I write "maybe" it underlines it, suggests I correct it by removing the "maybe."

If you shut one eye, depth disappears.

9.
I want to become legal again, and permanent. I tried
to draw a pinecone, distract myself with a manageable difficulty.

10.
What was it they asked you? *Why did you. . .* They couldn't connect the dots. *Why didn't you. . .* The story didn't line up.

11.
Having one-sided conversations is a form of madness. Devotion to an entity that cares
not for you is a delusion, which is another form of madness. Endless waiting is one more.
Anger, a madness. Grief.

12.
I once thought myself impervious to disaster, immune to loss.
Sure, bad things happened, but not to someone like me.

13.
Doppler effect as one way of understanding positionality: the siren's wail changes
depending on where you are in relation to its movement and on whether or not you
perceive yourself as arrestable, as unlawful, as the one whom it seeks.

14.
Loneliness: having no one to tell you stories about yourself.

15.
After many years of not wanting to, I decided to forgive my father, but the decision could
not be implemented for many years after.

16.

Virginia Woolf, describing how she felt upon seeing a performance of Chekhov's *The Cherry Orchard*: "... like a piano played upon at last, not in the middle only but all over the keyboard and with the lid left open so that the sound goes on."

17.

That skinless feeling. Your own endlessly permeable self.

# PANTOUM

New leaves, cold hands, the gray morning
promising rain. I might stay in a dream
of dead poets dying again: Táo Yuānmíng,
who I wake saying I must re-read.

Rain's tender promises stay in my dreams,
the pavement slick under the bike tire
from which I wake, saying I must read more Chinese,
unearth poems memorized from another millennium.

Slick pavement under my feet—
in the rain any place is a garden,
reciting soil from earlier millennia,
the same dirt that creases my nailbeds.

When it rains it is a garden everywhere,
like the field of red tulips where my mother poses,
the dirt creased in flowerbeds behind her
as vivid as the day my father took her photo.

The field of red tulips where my mother smiles
which I wake from, a vision of them together,
as sharp as if it were a photo—
her gray raincoat, his cold hands, new petals.

## OPEN LETTER TO THE BOY IN THE CAR

From a passing car, your voice lifts up and out,

                              calling. *Britney, Britney!*

A voice so high and smooth, it sounds like

singing—           *Britney!*

Like a ball tossed into the air that catches the light as it spins

into the right person's hands. For a moment, I want to greet

your voice with my own, but what is the other half of this song?

                                       Then I see you,

owner of the song-voice, your skin tender and white in the sun-

drugged afternoon. From the backseat of a sedan filled with

other boys just like you, you call the name again,

looking at me.                    And I recognize it, the tune snaps

into place: not the interpellation of friend, keen stranger,

not a mistake, but a mewling cat call.

                          Who *is* Britney?

                          How does a girl's name

                          become a weapon?

You can't be older than fourteen, hands cupped

around your mouth, skinny little wrists. Younger, must be,

than the boy who was a stepson to me, who will turn sixteen

this year, old enough to be inside this car, to be the one driving

who slows down so his friend can throw a girl's name

out the window, the window from which you—now

that you've dropped your hands and I see your pink

mouth—smile, seeing my confusion.

These days, the distance from heartbreak

to rage is so small, I am already giving you

the finger and walking away, hearing

your vulgar retort, still seeing in your face

the face of a boy I loved.

# STATE SYMBOLS

i.
What is the etymology of flesh—not the arrow of its trajectory to this mouth, but
something untended, blooming. We all know what can come from an omission, an om,
which is to say, a humming, a homing.

What were the sounds that surrounded you? Sounds you emulated: breath, teeth, tongue
hung, daggered in your mouth. Sounds embedded in your body (memorize, memorialize)
that linger, take hold. (*I pledge allegiance . . .*)

Someone else's mouth inside, trembling your membranes.

ii.
A single red flower. An abrasion of color.

Endless translation available: deep love, admiration, pity, a light
wounding.

*Sorry sorry sorry* the petals say in their feathery profusion. Or was it *happy birthday,
we're glad you survived, may your survivance be long, may you live past your own life
like these sewn stems—sown*? No, *sawn.*

Piece-meal mouth of a ghost incarnate. It is red. It drinks the water.
It says whatever it is we want it to say.

iii.
Hello, one who has been carved by the curved needles of cardinal cries in the rain.
This is your state bird. Famed for its redness (male), its omnipresence. We study it in our
reports and never learn its song.

A man I tried to love taught it to me. *This is their mating call.* Would his imitation draw
the birds from the air and to his mouth? *Now you try.* He drilled it into my ear until I
repeated it properly: two longs, five descents.

How to translate this song, when it has long been understood as *cheer cheer* and *birdie birdie birdie birdie birdie*? The rhythm thickens. The cardinals continue in the rain. *Rise? Rise? We-will-will-will-will-will.* Repeat after me: I pledge allegiance, to the flag, of the— *Rise? Rise?*

# WHILE YOU WERE GONE

*for Yusaku*

I moved through the rooms like a fish at the bottom of a darkened tank.

Finished the curry you made, spooning the thick brown sauce onto bread to mimic karepan.

Didn't go outside except to empty the vacuum cleaner's plastic tub.

The air was clammy as I lingered over our commingled detritus:

> hair
> black lint from your socks
> a few grains of rice
> gray fur of dead skin clinging to the filter

How many times have we compared our faces, forearms, and bellies in the bathroom mirror after a shower. Here in the vacuum, we were both pale as dust.

The shed surfaces of us shot into the air like spores from a puffball and speckled the matted grass.

The snow all gone, melted almost overnight.

On the lawn, dark mossy clumps of my hair from when you cut it and dumped it outside, hoping birds would use the strands.

It was not the right season for nest building.

Still, you came back. Called it *home.*

# AT THE MILLER HOUSE

Columbus, Indiana

*Notice the theme of floating,* our volunteer guide says, pointing to the light gray exterior walls. We take out our phones to capture the weeping European beech—the first of its kind I've seen—dangling dark papery leaves in cascading caves to mark the walkway into the house. On the drive up

she was already upset. *All of this for just one family?* she scoffed when I showed her the tickets. *Why should I care about this?* Now we are separated by the other tourists who look back and forth between us, not sure if we belong together. *You can't take*

*pictures inside,* so we snap the arborvitae at the property edge, shoot the driveway cobbled with puzzle-piece terra-cotta.

Inside, it is marble, chilled. *Notice the carpet, a perfect replica of the original.* This the first famous house where I've been let in. *What a dream.* 360-degree fireplace and a conversation pit, the cushion colors of which would be switched according to season. We shuffle through

the rooms, rotating our bodies to see it all again: the golds and greens and peacock blues. I don't know the names for any of these things except what the guide tells me: *primitive figurines collected by Mr. Miller, folk art* next to a glass piece that *won an award at the Venice Biennale.*

The glossy kitchen where Mrs. Miller herself clearly never cooked, island cabinets being exactly face-level to hide the expression of the one cooking or cleaning on the other side. To see the other side

of a room, my mother steps off the beige runner and onto the stone floor and the guide stops mid-sentence to remind her to *please stay on the marked path.* Everyone—the rest of us who have no trouble staying where we are told—turns and looks. My own irritation

I muzzle by staring into the chandelier. The house and its light, a room for each of the children. The empty wall where Monet water lilies once hung.

Then we come to the piano. *Look closer, isn't it a bit longer than your regular Steinway baby grand*? *And look*, someone had painted the underside a deep red. For my first five years in this country, I played a tinny keyboard. Then my mother bought a one-hundred-year-old spinet

from a church yard sale. We sanded its varnish-flecked body smooth and painted it baby blue. It never held its tune, but it played, notes leaking into each other, filling the apartment with sound. *Don't worry,* I want to tell her now, softening, *there's a museum for that, too.*

# ON INJURY

For most of the movie,

      I had been aware of my need to urinate but even more aware of the entire row of
people's laps I'd have to crab-leg across to do so, so I stayed in my seat, putting
other people's imagined discomfort ahead of my own bodily functions,

          but I also didn't want to miss any portion of the movie that I was so eager
to see, which was turning out to be a good one despite the fact that I had
managed hurt my wrist right before from sporting with friends, knowing
only the vaguest things about stopping the white ball when it came in my
direction with, of all things, my forearms, and the wrist was swollen hot
and bright pink (anyone else might have stopped playing until several
more hours' worth of instructional YouTube videos had been viewed),
which meant it would throb every so often—like when I shifted in my
seat to get a clearer view—and kept me from holding hands with Y, which
we often do when we watch movies, an act that helps someone like me
with an overactive imagination to stay rooted to this life in this body,

so when the movie was over and the lights went up, I rushed downstairs to the
bathroom, and, having relieved myself, came back to find everyone dispersing
into the cold evening (I love that feeling of emerging from a theater and into the
now-dark day, as if what we'd seen made it so), and we made our farewells to the
friends who'd sat beside us for the last two hours and with whom we now shared
the lives of those depicted on screen: the light on the actors' facesfrom the porch
as they looked up into their night sky empty of the fireworks they could hear but
not see, the crunch in their mouths of korokke, deep fried to perfection, the final
wrenching separation of the ad hoc but very real family,

after which Y and I walked back to the car and I said something I didn't quite mean like
*how sad* and then tears that I hadn't realized I'd been holding were there, hot on my face,
reminding me how strange weeping can be, how one injury becomes connected with others
and in our bodies can be metabolized then released together, how witnessing fictive pain
can activate our own dormant sensitivities—and now, two weeks later, the bruise I knew
was there from the ball hitting my wrist has finally surfaced from the deeper tissue, as if it
will eventually float up and through my skin into the air.

# 连翘

*Forsythia suspensa, or weeping
forsythia: a flowering shrub taken
from China by European botanists,
who gave it another name.*

My father pushes the bike
as I sit, legs dangling,
too short to ride.

It has just rained, the air
cool under the 梧桐 trees,
and streetlamps canopy

the darkness with yellow light.
I don't remember where
we are going, if this is a dream.

Now I bike home alone
in the Bloomington night,
moisture like a warm palm

against my forehead,
branches of honeysuckle
dripping over the grass.

For years after I left 西安,
I mistook honeysuckle
for 连翘 and gave its nectared

scent to my weeping native
plant, which is itself scentless.
This kind of false attribution

has its uses. Pushing my face
into a feathery spray, it is spring
in 西安 and the air is blossoming

               with rain—

# AUTOSCOPY

woken by rain on the wútóng trees

outside     someone drags a dustpan
collecting all that we've relinquished

in the courtyard          past the silver
ginkgo and rosebushes

Wàigōng counts his steps
from his lips     a trail of nightbreath

escaping          with my eyes closed
the second skin of heat clinging to me

is the body I used once
and abandoned          it lingers still

in the long avenues     under the leaves

materializing where the rain touches
letting me approach    the iron gate

where memory waits

# Notes

" . . . loss and grief are generated by juridicopolitical mechanisms . . . "
(page 29)

> Title is a quote from *Racial Melancholia, Racial Dissociation* by David
> L. Eng and Shinhee Han.

"Shape Note" (page 46)

> Lyrics are from "Idumea" from *The Sacred Harp* songbook.
> The play was written by Peter Schumann and performed by Bread and
> Puppet Theater in the summer of 2013, with lines taken from *The
> Baghavad Gita*.

"Entries from the Hottest Year on Record" (page 61)

> Virginia Woolf quote as recorded in my journal, from her essay "The
> Russian Point of View."

"连翘" (page 75)

连翘 is pronounced lián qiáo.

梧桐 is wútóng (see below).

西安 is my birth city and namesake, Xī'ān.

"Autoscopy" (page 77)

> Wútóng is the Chinese name for the *Firmiana simplex*, which
> is known for its resonant wood, which is used to make musical
> instruments, as well as coffins.

> Wútóng is also a name for the French-introduced *Platanus ×
> acerifolia*, or plane tree, which is tolerant of subpar conditions and
> therefore frequently used as a roadside shade tree.

> Wútóng trees are where phoenixes are said to alight, and the word
> itself is also a slant homonym for wú tòng: *without pain* or *without
> sorrow*.

# Acknowledgments

Many thanks to the editors at the following journals where these poems first appeared:

*The Arkansas International*: "Remains" (as "Tracks")
*Cream City Review*: "While You Were Gone"; "连翘"
*The Cincinnati Review miCRo:* "On Injury"
*Ecotone*: "Ditch"
*The Georgia Review*: "The Story"; "Additionally, what freedoms have I been trained to deny myself?"; "Xī'ān Nocturne with Jasmine and Pears"; "Demolished Landscape with Open Mouth"; "Memory in a Foreign Language"
*Grist Journal*: "Six years old, my classmates and I"; "On Jay Peak Road"
*Hyphen*: "Finding Fruit"; "Misapprehension"
*The Journal*: "Solstice"
*Pleaides*: "Night Swim at Shadow Lake"
*Ploughshares*: "What No One Told You"; "Entries from the Hottest Year on Record"
*Poetry*: "Going Back"; "State Symbols"; "At the Miller House"; "Jiangsu, Early Summer"
*The Margins* (AAWW): "Ars Poetica in a Dream Language"
*Quarterly West*: "Northeast Kingdom"
*Sonora Review*: "Hypnogogia" (as "What I Will Leave")
*Third Coast*: "Upon Hearing the News"

I was first tasked with writing acknowledgments in a workshop hosted by Ross Gay, and instead I wrote an essay about obligatory gratitude and agency, an essay that seethed. I was practicing resistance in the fall of 2017, and training a willful voice against the obedience instilled in me. This is not that essay, and the thing I wonder at the most is how easily gratitude comes now, and how it allows for a different kind of disobedience.

Thanks to my teachers, especially my teachers of poetry: David Caplan, Robert Olmstead, Denise Duhamel, Lynette Carpenter, Michelle Disler, Allison Joseph, Robert Hass, A. E. Stallings, Amber Flora Thomas,

Romayne Dorsey, Catherine Bowman, Stacey Lynn Brown, Adrian Matijka, Walton Muyumba, Nikki Skillman, Bill Johnston, for being friends and guides lighting the path.

Thanks to my early readers. To OWU writers and P&J'ers for beginning and staying with me, especially Martha Park and Abby Dockter. To my IU MFA crew—and especially to my "coho"—whose feedback and ideas were indispensable. To Danni Quintos, Lisa Low, and Su Cho for hot tub retreats and hot ideas. To the Undocupoets, for the joyous chorus of your company, and to Janine Joseph, for opening that first door. To The Mae Fellowship— Courtney and Lindsay—and to the second cohort for your generosity and collective brilliance. To the (unofficial) Minneapolis Institute of Art Writers and to Gao Vang for gathering us in the Before, and to the After. Finally and especially to Lisa Low, for being the best book buddy one could ask for.

For their support: The American Literary Translators Association, Bread Loaf Environmental Writers' Conference, The National Society for the Arts, The Anderson Center, The Mae Fellowship, and The Civitella Ranieri Foundation.

Bottomless thanks to Gabe Fried and everyone at team Persea for granting wishes with such care and attentiveness, and to the Persea poets who precede and surround me: what a delight to be amongst you.

For coworkers and authors at Graywolf Press, for all the books that raised me and for the books I now have a hand in, many howls of joy for that.

For Bread & Puppet Theater and all the joy of making I encountered there. For Maria and Josh and Cate Hill Orchard for a most magical season of apples, sheep, and song.

For my friends, true muses who have held me at my worst and celebrated me at my best (and vice versa): Hannah, Alex, Kassel, Gabe, Pat, Yvet, all the once and forever bandmembers of Taiyoka, Brianna, Soleil, Irene, Morgan, Casey, Anna and Grant (plus Tig and Sugi!).

For Yusaku, who read every version—thank you for building a life with me that can hold poetry, jam sessions, tennis, tea, and days-long philosophical debates. Thank you for recognizing my ancestors in me, for that long-sighted kind of love.

For my chosen family on Randall Avenue and Bantry Street, who have been the "who else" who held me from even before that first landing in Detroit, who have been there ever since.

For my family in China. What a marvel to be your descendant, to inherit your bodies in my own. I have been lucky to be a child of many grandparents, and this is for them, for their xīn téng. For my dad, nearer every day. For my mom, who plucked me from the moon and raised me in apartments full of books and music, who read these poems with such generosity and imagination—thank you, I love you.

Finally, for anyone who has listened to or read my poems, and anyone who has shared their poetry with me. All of this will never not astonish me. To the singing, as it keeps moving through us.

# About the Author

ANNI LIU (刘安妮) was born in Xī'ān, Shǎnxī, (西安, 陕西) in the year of the goat. Shortly before the new millennium, she emigrated to Bowling Green, Ohio, where she grew up in libraries. Her work is featured in *Poetry* magazine, *Ploughshares*, *Ecotone*, *Columbia Journal*, *Two Lines*, and elsewhere, and her honors include an Undocupoets Fellowship, a Katherine Bakeless Nason Scholarship to Bread Loaf Environmental Conference, a National Society for Arts and Letters' Literature Award, and a Mae Fellowship. She earned her MFA from Indiana University, where she served as poetry editor of *Indiana Review*. She is working on a hybrid memoir about parole, translating the poetry of Dù Yá (度涯), and editing fiction and nonfiction at Graywolf Press. Inquiries for collaboration are welcome. Find her online at anniliuwrites.wordpress.com.